Made in the USA
Las Vegas, NV
05 March 2025

19068207R10056